Met*a*mor*pho*sis

A Book of Poetry

Lizy J. Campbell

Dedication

To all those who struggle in life for those days to find your smile, you are not alone. We are all in this together, hold on; It does get better.

You are enough.

About This Book

Over the years, experiences and changes in my life have driven me to write poetry.

Some are reflective of my life, and some are feelings of things I have seen and pain of others, that I have captured on paper. It is an interpretation yet not defined by anyone thing or being.

Whether it had impacted me to change into the person I am now, or if it was a part of my evolution, I don't have the answer.

It is a sort of therapy, a release, to let go of wounds and circumstance that define who I am today. I am still a work in progress.

Therefore, a metamorphosis of life. Enjoy.

The Wolf

The wolf in sheep's clothing
All knowing
Eyes are Glowing
Teeth aren't showing
Victim is near
They can sense the fear
It makes them drool with glee
Knowing you won't get the chance to flee
Ready to pounce
Making you shutter with every ounce
Closer they watch
Cunning like a fox
Teeth displayed
you cannot get away, frayed
Grab hold
Unsuspected
You, now cold
Truths stripped bare
Life can be unfair
The wolf knows no feeling
Its place is in the unbelieving
Devilish glare, its heart never fills
Of unsuspecting little kills
Beware of the Wolf in sheep's clothing,
it knows no truth in life, and is growing
Run now before it begins to start showing
The Wolf

Dark Heart

Soul of light or darkness
I don't know its difference

You see me, you try to stomp it
I felt it, there was no doubt

You told me nothing's there
You will feel my pain, and its more than you can bare

Ignore it more
Push and shove it far

Dark and empty, you like it that way
I don't even try cause your pull never fails to play
Keep me on a shelf until your ready to use
Hurt me more, try to get me to stay

Dark heart, you use us as pawns
until we lost our crowns

Keep us on a leash
Keeping us from speech

Darkened heart
You finally suffocated me

Getting over you,
its the only thing I can do to be free

Dreamer

Keeper of the dream sanctuary
Remind me of things reality can't give me
Exit out those diamond eyes
Shine like stars that gleam on my face
Safe within the clouds around my head
Sleeping on a feather bed of lies
When I wake up I am afraid
I dealt the devils cards today
Sleep is the only escape
Carry me away
In the cloud's I play
Safely with you
I would pass the time away
Give me more of the dreams when I wake
Turn around, eyes open
Don't stop dreaming,
in the day

Trouble

You walked in the door and I knew
Trouble
You smiled and I fell to the floor
Trouble
My head started to spin
Trouble
I knew I fell for it again
Trouble
His charm had me shaking
Trouble
I felt as if he talked like a poet in the making
Trouble
I just want to dance he held his hand out
Trouble
I just want to drive you home he said
Trouble
Left me wanting more
Trouble
He walked me to the door
Trouble
He kissed me once more
Trouble
His embrace felt like I was adored

I knew I was in trouble

Outside

I thought of you every second of the day
I tried to overcompensate
The fear cut into me deeper then death looked me in the
face
So I opened up, or so I thought
Choked, and swallowed, drowned in loss
Grabbing a love that was conditional
Then all of a sudden, I'm on the outside looking in
Looking off in the distance of another set of memories
Only thing that I have left to hold onto
Those days, when you wanted
Hell bent, keep me at arms length
Like I never meant anything
As though you thought I never felt what it was like to be on
the inside
You managed to hurt me again
Different, like your trying to push me away
More and more little by little, every day
It so cold on the outside
It's as though hearts have turned into stone
Never gave me a valid reason
Pulled out the knife you thrust in my chest
Always under a condition
Outside once again, where the world is in shambles
No one knows how to show love for one another
Everyone has pain but, no one talks about how to fix it
Leave each other instead
No one wants to fix things, just get new toys to play with
They all end up the same way
On the outside looking in

I lost her

I felt this pull from the day you came into my life
Something, it always vibrated in me

Took you to things to take your mind away
Hoping that you would find happiness
and stay a little while longer
That smile, sometimes only lasted for minutes

I thought if I kept pushing it away,
I could keep it far from you
Keep this dark cloud from taking over
From this mental health that screwed us over

I lost her

She was swallowed whole by darkness,
the Depression, the last straw, had finally hooked her
I couldn't hold it back any longer
The monster had come for her

Nothing has been the same since
She hates me now more than ever,
because I didn't save her, from herself

Now she's a product of mental health
It was just another word,
it didn't save her from her destination

Doctors are fighting to give her another diagnosis

I lost her (cont'd)

she sits alone with her monsters, and bottles of pills,
even now,
and I am left with one less hand to hold
She's lost within her mind

I wonder if the world will ever catch up,
to save the lost girl,
which mental health took

Spit it out

Times are hard, but worse is this still
are the times we never remember,
to just let our emotions spill
Flow them out like a river bed
Never leaving anything unspoken, unsaid
Instead we leave those words for dead
Let them eat us alive inside our head
We just aren't built that way
We are so jaded
We sabotage our happiness, daily
Then regret it, funny isn't it?
Waiting for the time to spit them out like a poison,
to twist those words we heard in our head
To violate and defeat and make others feel small
Never knowing its us who feels like no one at all
Spit out those words till you feel like less,
in the end, it wasn't worth the breath
Now scars are present instead

Pull

Pulling me from so far
Your soul shines like a star
I feel the darkness within you
Sometimes I have even felt it too
I touch your face
I am just a ghost you try to replace
Yet you pull me like I'm tied to you
Tied to your heart
This string is nothing new
Can't fight it anymore
The pull of you

Luminescence

Euphoric light
Happiness guiding divine

Glow and funnel it
Catch the spirit of it

Luminescent energy
it radiates to me

Positive Light
Catching flight

Subatomic motions
Brighten the soul notions

Vanquish Negativity
Cords that were attached to me

Feel the Electra-luminescence
it has presence

Be the light people need to see
Gather up and decide to be

Stand up as one
a unity

Give

Give them something to remember
Give them your best
Give them your gift

Give them it
Never let them forget

Give me what I gave
Give me your best
Give me I am obsessed

Give me peace
Give me love
Give me what I give you in my chest

Give it your all
Give me forgiveness

Give them memories
Give them a love that no one will protest

Give me what You want
But never take my love and put it to rest

What money cannot buy

What money can't buy
Is the sight of your child's smile

What money can't buy
The air we breathe

What money can't buy
Is a home with peace

What money can't buy
That soul that is lost

What money can buy
is material thing's

Keep buying it all to fill the emptied heart

Money is not evil
it's used for good

What money can't buy, is a good person who would

Hang on

Lean your head on my heart
Even though we are far apart
I whisper in your ear
have no fear
I won't let you down
Now that you are found
Hang on to me,
I will be your energy
I won't let a day go,
without letting you know
Happiness is the key
Keep your positivity
You can fly
To the moon with me
hang on to me

Brown Eyes

Those brown eyes
have seen the darkest skies

Have risen above it all
Just to watch them crawl

The ones that took the first swing
Fists flying
Trying to keep her from being

Brown eyes have damages now
They saw too much
blow by blow

Brown eyes
wipe those tears
Its gone
no more good byes

Brown eyes
Twinkles still
Even if the heart is pained

No one can ever take her down
She won't be anyone's clown

Brown eyes
Look up to the skies
Their is a light above you

Brown Eyes (cont'd)

No one here but you
to save you

Brown eyes
You are stronger than you know

Never let anyone take
the spark you make

Brown eyes
You will never compromise

Motivation

Need some motivation
Dark days I saw then
But I fought and won them

My motivation
It's like a steady soft glow
Like the moon upon a pillow

Show me the light
Keeping my line of sight

The motivation grows
This you'd have to know

How to feel quite dead
To now appreciate the unsaid

Its connection to the soul
That's the motivation
that found my soul

Motivated by past pain
Never wanting it to come again

Like a soft glow
Of the moon above my pillow

Miss you

Miss you
The tears fall like rain
Here I go
I'm thinking of him, again

Miss you
I hold on to the pain
Its all that remains
the thoughts of you
I'm going insane

I miss you
your voice
That intelligence
That humour
That handsome face

Gimme a moment
Watching the moon, shine on
I wonder if you feel it this strong
Angel, I need you by my side
To whisper in his ear
Tell him I miss him,
want him near

Miss you
My favourite thing that's not here
Touch your forehead
kiss you there

Miss you (cont'd)

Silky smooth skin
Making me tingle again

Reach out and getting nothing but air

Miss you,
want you near
Bring him here

Miss you
I'm the angel, whispers
I feel you,
have no fear
She wasn't for you
You're lost, and I found you

You need to come to the moon
I been waiting here

Monsters out there

Not all monsters are out there
There are people that care

People who bend down,
to give the last bit of change out

People who remove shoes for those who have none, and
are tapped out

There is monsters out there,
but good people are everywhere

Ones who give seats to those who can't stand,
gives donations when they can

Saves the lives of those who cannot speak,
gives time, helps the meek

Monsters beware, good people are everywhere

So, even though many have no name
Remember every helping hand is so much for so little

It's free to be kind and gentle

Pay it forward, everyday
In every way

Will you remember

Will you remember me
When I am old and can't see
Will you remember me
My laugh so loud, it was full of life
That's me
Will you remember me
A big heart that gave too much of me
Will you remember me
All the things that I did for free
Will you remember me
Strong, even though so much was taken out of me
Will you remember me and come to visit me
Will you remember me
The sacrifice I made, constantly
Will you remember me
All the love I gave, you took a part of me
Will you remember me

Three faces of me

Three faces of me
Which one do you see

Do you see the strong one, who never gives up
Do you see the sensitive one, who cares too much
Do you see the lost one, who keeps starring at the moon

Three faces of me
Lost am I, because you left me

Do you see the lies you told, hurt me
Do you see the cover up that holds me
Do you see the lines of life has told me

Three faces of me
I am holding on to keep myself seen

The three faces of me starring at the moon
Do you see me?

How did this come about,
that I am always stressed out

As a kid, I had worry
Now, I can't even enjoy a day out

Three Faces of me

(cont'd)

How did I get like this,
was it the hard life I did not wish

Now. I am older and wiser still,
but it hasn't helped pay the bill

How did time escape my life
One minute ago I was a wife

Now a mom for life,
the greatest love of mine is only three feet tall

How did I get so blessed
Even with all this stress

It's them that I worry
How life goes so fast and blurry

I am so privileged
I have purpose and so I see

Nothing matters but them
And its a great life I lead

They were meant for me
How did I get so lucky, how?

Love within

I loved myself today
turned him down so I would stay

I found my love from within
It was in me, not in him

Thought I loved him,
turns out I love me just a little bit more

Figured this out before I am old
Loving myself is worth more then gold

I finally found the love within

Forgiveness

Forgive you,
though I wont forget

You gave me reason to regret

Forgave the past, and its demons with it

Lessons taught
Now I have grown

Stronger still
Cautious like a stone

Unwavering philosophy,
about how I want things to be

Forgive them for they are weak
Knowing no boundaries,
it is the sick they seek

Understanding is what they need
But not foolish trust to, just believe

Forgive,
let the lesson serve as a guide
Never to let that road cross your path

Independence,
to love yourself again,
that no one will ever make you feel like less then, them

Free

Letting go to the memory of you
free
Moving on and being happy
free
Letting go of the thought of you looking at the moon like
me
free
Souls will meet again I am sure but 'til then
free
Pain of yesterday
free
Let it be
Free
Need to expand and spread my wings
I need to be
Free

Hide

Hide your eyes
Cause you can't see it

Tell everyone to hide
Cause your lies can't achieve it

Make excuses
Hide behind screens, and fake it

Tell her to block it out
Hide the lies, cause you cannot take it

Hide inside the idea
cause you can't cope with it

Make up stories about it
Hide your lies, cause no one will like it

Cut them off, so no one will find it

Pretend everyone else is crazy, so you can live with it

Hide the truth, so you can keep pretending it
Make excuses, so you can live with it

Hiding out the obligation,
you will never have to face it

Hide (cont'd)

Just hide from life

Keep faking it

Wake up!

Hiding lies will not last for long

Days, months, years, it will not be long

Hide your lies, until you're wrong

Beast of Belief

Ripped my heart out
Take it,
frozen

A wasted time and feeling for,
bleeding on the floor
No one wants it anymore

I am in dismay
I am another scar you adore
No I won't be your little whore
Something to abuse
and use
NO not any more

Frighten me,
those fangs stained red
You want to make me bleed, instead?
You thought I would let you in
Instead I show you what I am made of
I stand firm

Wiped the tears away
Don't show them,
it will be okay

Beast of Belief (cont'd)

I have fangs of my own
Not afraid of the devils face
I will jump and chase
Get out of my way
Fear is not welcome here today

The demons fear love
Hate it and want to separate it
Recoil in the thought of it
Faith the greatest weapon

I am a beast of belief
I never question

Fade out, you wicked feeling
You're not welcome here anymore
Don't come again
Fear, will not darken my door

Let it go

Let it go
It serves no purpose
Holding on to ghosts
Giving her opportunity

I smell her perfume
I sense her near
She's stealing your essence
The darkness
Toxic energy
Keep talking
Talk till you won't figure it out
Leaving you empty
Forever lost
Set yourself free
Choked out by guilt
So weak, but very unhealthy
Sadness
Yet a danger to ones reality
Get out!
Leave, before you have nothing left
Save yourself
Find passion for breathing life
Nothing less
Get obsessed
Find light
Live

Let it go (cont'd)

Breathe
You will be OK
Law of attraction

This law you cannot see
It vibrates through you and me
It makes the universe listen
It brings us back to what we ought to be

Positive is the key

Give your vision a chance
You may become part of a great new Dance
Thoughts are things not yet into play
So be careful what you say

Dreams

Close my eyes...

Feel the sand between my toes

The laughter heard and sun on my skin

The joy, it comes from within

Listen to the waves crashing down

Palm trees dancing among the clouds

A time when I was young

When she gave me kisses and loved me so

A kindness, never let it go

Her voice still inside my head

I woke, and realized it was just in my dream

She was still calling me

Told me to go to my family

They needed me

Tell You

When I got home, I wanted to tell you
But I put it on pause
You argued with me all night without cause

Now I am only tired and forgot to tell you

I left for work, and I wanted to tell you
But when I leaned in to kiss your lips
You shrank away and gave me dirty looks

The days became weeks and I forgot to tell you
Exactly what I was meaning to say
It did not matter anyway

I did not feel like I did that day

I somehow lost those words I wanted to say
I feel like it does not even matter now anyway
Now I just want to get away

Leave, get out, be free of you

The words I wanted to tell you
they are different from what I had in my mind
Now I just want to keep silent

Tell You (cont'd)

I just want it finished with you
I just wanted to tell you that I have fallen out of love
with you
Its sad because those are not the words, I had wanted
to tell you

Now I do not ever remember wanting to tell you.

One minute of fame

At its most
At its best
At the place of remarkable success

At its peak
At its prime
Cutting edge and fame sublime

At a glimpse
Out of time
It was all a waste of time

Moments

Dancing in the breeze
Oh, what a beautiful feeling to me

Singing my favourite song
I want to hear it all night long

Talking to my best friend on the phone
I love the feeling that I am not alone

Playing with my lover in the sand
I just want to be with him, holding his hand

Dreaming of things in my sleep
I will find it and make it mine to keep

Touch me, make me believe
Kiss me and set me free

Pull me in, give me a new light
Give me a love I want to fight

Discover truths that I need to hear
Hold me close, I will never fear

Give me strength darling,
you make this moment worth it,
loving you

Good-bye

Goodbye,
whispers near
Soon it is time,
the time we all never expect,
we remain to view now
Your light growing dim
For the love of one,
is what comes through
Even if it means seeing so little of what was left
Nothing is harder to say,
nothing harder to hear,
your human form is no more
Cannot see your smile,
hear your voice
I will not say it
I refuse,
will it make you stay here?
I shut my mouth and pray it will never happen
I know I have no choice,
it is your time to phase out
The light must reach the stars now
Become one with the universe,
but I will keep you in my heart
Love you forever
Good-bye, is all I can mutter

One Man

He was just one man in this universe
He loved a few
He was not famous
His voice fell silent
No one else knew
One man
no one else saw
The love he gave his family
The things he did
One man
his life is leaving now
This person I knew
Did not have to be famous
did not have to be well known
He was just my uncle
He just loved me
Thank you for being you
That one man showed me
Family

Dedicated to my Uncle Stewart Dobson

You (Micro Poetry)

Silence is deafening

Whispers in the night

Constant reminder of things

things that never took flight

Darkness, hugs tight

Tears fall where they may

Good night

Words

Words hurt,
they cut like diamonds
No need for violence,
the wound is large
Words spoken,
like a missile launched
Thoughtless mind,
words remain
Ingrained
No sorry will fix it
Betrayed by words
The information contained
Cut off the oxygen
So unkind
Yet you remain
Words
That is all that is left
Like the remains of a string
These words hurt me
Now, I leave
And no ones here
Because I let it get to me
Your ugly words
Thoughtless
Unhinged
Now all that is left
Are those words
.... you spoke

Call

Call it friend
Call it, text it
Pretend

Call it less
Call it lies

Call it only when you need me
Then cries

Call it no more
Calling is a chore

Call you later
Call you no more

Call you?
I do not know you anymore

The Watcher

A watcher in the distance
Emotionally charged stares
Thinking of sending a message out
Keep a close eye out
I feel those glares

Watching
But it is far too late
Watch me as I walk away
Never looking back on yesterday
Watch your own life pass

Thinking of the days when life was grand
Then I took a stand
So, keep watching me
I am happy
Everyday is better than before
Nothing you did will ever stop me
You and I are no more

Watch in the darkness of your mess
The creation of lies and filth, you sit with unrest

I am full of light
A place you cannot see
The watcher is blind

And I am set free

Internet Love Beware

Staring at your computer screen
reading her stats, take the information
waiting for a time of attack,
sad and lonely

Perfect, he had his new escapade
Unsuspected, she took the bait
He called it fate

He lies in wait
Behind the screen
Never meeting
Evading
His intense loving heart break
Pretending to be all that you need
A cyber real man, indeed

Reeling her in
She decides to let him in
Closer she reveals all that she is
He has gotten her and now its time for the kill
He ghosts her and fades out

Pretending now,
so busy, is all he would say
A big life you have now,
do not have time today

Internet Love Beware (cont'd)

Now tears fall from all the lies
He tricked her,
another cyber got to her
Its a game they play

Internet love, beware

I am an Artist

I am an artist
its not what someone said I would be
It's who I am
It's the very fabric of me
It's my Aura, deep within
Bleeding out ideas with my pen
Cry out, my hand it needs to express
So, a piece released into this place
To set it free
To be visually, on the right frequency
So, you can try understanding me?
I am an artist
I paint my world in diverse ways,
see me from places unknown
My perspective is always a blur,
its paint that creates
Makes it clear
You may not understand me,
I am okay with that
An artists life is a beautiful mess of colour

I did

I did, I loved you
But it was not fair

You told me things
You said to every girl out there

Made me think,
I am just a fling

A blinking light
A hollow kindness

A space in your place
Going nowhere

Crashing on your shadow of despair
Constantly changing, the games you play

I did, I loved you
But love is not enough

I am and never will be, the only
Cause you just wait till you find another

Replaced

Liquid Shrink

Liquid killer, you drink to hide
The pain of it
So, you decide
You use it to comfort,
bottle down
Drink those emotions,
kill those thoughts
Drink to obliterate,
numb
Headache is remembering
Cannot hide forever
Liquids never last,
once its out of your system
Killing to forget
Liquid shrink,
does not have the answers
It only makes you sick

Begin

Put my heart all in
Waiting for it to begin

Knocked down, but I stand up again

No problem
I am starting again

Fell
Tomorrow, I will do it all over

Today, I will win
I will never give in

Its a flicker of faith that keeps me going,
sets me up for a win

It has already begun
I am ready this is it

Grab it, and never let go
My thoughts are already winning

Time for new beginning

Miss

Miss the banter
Miss the conversation
Miss the calm with no altercation
Miss the what ifs
Miss the times you always slept
Miss it
Miss us
Miss this
Miss this place
Miss the embrace
Miss the person I dreamed; I thought you were
Miss the thoughts of a fantasy world, that was never there
Miss the kiss
Miss the fake promises
Miss the idea of pretending life was great

Miss nothing now

Missing you, I forgot

Psychopath

Lure me in without a doubt, you are a pro
Give me love then you do not need me now I know
Pull on my emotions play on my feelings
Make me feel like I am crazy
But that was your strategy
Complain others are not so nice,
then you are out telling everything
they are your ex, but they are so great now, oh, so nice
Snatch my insecurities, watch as a puppet of yours I
became
Saying so many gives you what I cannot,
that is not what you made me think before
You told me I was all you want, and nothing more
Fool I was, for I had no chance
I am giving, and you like a cat, had to pounce
But now I see you, clear,
the deviant
The one who has no heart, I will not shed a tear
The psychopath that creates pain, and that's a fact
Never again, I will not fall for that trap
This time I will watch and remember this dance
Hold on and bat knowledge,
knock out any who play this tune
Now I will not be a slave to the psychopath

Silence

So quiet, here I am grabbing

But I get nothing but air

Silence, cuts me like a knife

Feeling less

Without breathing your air,

standing still

Not a sound came out,

waiting for something,

anything

For you to just care

Stars

What if we were stars bursting and twisted, made human
Piece of us went in another direction,
magnetized it pulls us we are forever searching
Trying to find our others half or missing piece
What if we no matter where or even the distance it to be
whole
To see ourselves; to feel other's feelings
To find this energy
Something that would make us happy,
who creates this inner peace
This other human who gets us completely,
searching this magnetic force that drew you here
My heart is open, and my mind is clear
Just waiting till I see you here

Tell Them

Tell them stories keep them entertained

Tell them lies, keep them blind and framed, pressed in

Tell them dreams and keep them floating above the sky

Tell them the truth, let them decide

Tell them quietly, but try not to shatter their pride

Just tell them something, to not think the worst

Tell them not what they want to, but something that hurt

The Galaxy Is Calling

The galaxy is calling
days I wait, tears I cry
I will wait till I am old and die...
Cause I saw a diamond in those eyes
I was a lost soul and then I met someone like you
Precious please do not let go of the dream
I will not let go of you
Reaching out for someone I cannot see
In darkness I will pull you safety
God only knows the reason
He was meant for me to see him
searching for the meaning
I his beacon
Are not there enough of us among the moons
That he picked me for you
It does not matter
I decided this is something I want to do
I will save you

Toy

Played me took my heart out
bounced it on the floor
thought it was a toy and nothing more

Left me in silence
Robbed me of your time
Left me in the shadows
This is how it goes

Like the toys of a child, it grows tired of play
the novelty wore off, you had enough of it today
Cannot get the dust off
Something to dispose of
Toy heart is just that,
throw it out,
and just forget about it
Played like a toy,
all used up,
thrown out

Eyes

Eyes, I see into your soul

Eyes, I can tell your sorrow

I see your energy

Eyes, the pain you cannot hide

Eyes, I see through you

Eyes, saw so much before me

Eyes, that love to see the beauty

Eyes, I see me

Eyes, are my window into destiny

Patience

Patience, is what I will do for thee
Patience, is waiting for you to show me

Patience, is the calm that overtakes me
Patience, is my gift and love for you
Patience, I will wait forever for you
Patience, to know that I can wait to show you

Patience, is my trust

I only have eyes for you
I know to love you, patience is necessary,
my patience is power
I will save thee
Patience, is the thing that saves me
waiting patiently for you,
to hold you in my arms
To look into your eyes
To be one patiently,
my heart complete
I am patient

Alone

I am alone, I am not sad
I am alone, and I am satisfied
I am alone, its nice the quiet
I am alone, but I feel love all around and like it

I am alone, and I like the company I keep
I am alone, and I like me
Not all can say this freely
People need to have someone, or are they empty?

If you cannot be alone with yourself
How can you be with anyone else?
I am alone, so I say but are we really?
No one is ever alone truly

Sea of Disappointment

It was all your intention
To make me fall in, then throw me back to the sea
In shark infested waters amongst the fish
You bit till I bled out
Swimming amongst the others, you have no radiance, only sadness
 Just scars that pass along and infect the waters, pleading I was once happy
Twist and turn, you are like a fish, then bubble forth heartache
Everything you touch is like a hook that catches your prey
I am diving for your treasure, saying you are not here for anything, so I will fade out
The sea has always been chilly, and I must get out
Floating away until the net of darkness catches up with me
Till then, I remain still,
in the sea disappointment

Seize the Moment

Did you get this opportunity before?

Someone who did something out of the ordinary,
so much more

Did you grab it by the reigns, or let it slip away?

Did you shut it down for fear it might not work out?

We are all just a decision away,

from something great or something tragic,

while we work it out in out minds did the moment pass or,
fade to grey,

Do you regret it and wish it were different today maybe it
is time to follow?
a gift given to you,

it is time to take a chance

We only have one life to live,

so, live it

Virtual Friend

I am just an app on your phone

A window to close

A cyber friend

An extension of your friends you never met

Electronic devices are where I remain

In your pocket

A little singular jolt of electronic
mischief

A lid to close

A click away to shut off

No one of consequence

The Forces of Life

Pulling stronger the force with no name
Strange I feel your energy from a million miles away
Feel your presence strong and calling
Its growing increasingly,
getting closer than I could ever expect
Come here
Intense feelings keep growing,
how was I supposed to know?
Cannot escape it
 I do not want it to leave me now
Fate, is it knocking?
I will open the door
I welcomed you, and do not ask for more
Everything happens for a reason, so they say
Under the same stars, souls never know distance
Someday, you will be standing beside me
We will heal each other's previous broken shards of
heartbreak
You are my other side of the moon,
destiny
Wonderful gentle ripple in the sea
Forces of us in a world amongst millions,
a beacon lighthouse of your hearts, calling home

Friendship

Treat yourself as a treasure
You deserve so much better
Ignorance, is bliss
Only if its not the friends, you dismiss
Keep up plastic appearances
friends that come and go,
knowing only true ones are few
Someone who cares they say will always be there
But do not take advantage
For damages you may not be able to repair
Friendship takes care,
lies and distrust you cannot spare
In the end its the real human connection that binds
The friends that are there that matter
They rejuvenate your spiritual core

Chance

Do not let go

Died for just a second to catch my breath

Insecure give it a chance
Hold on to what brought you here

Just wait while I catch up

Damaged healing
still licking my wounds

Understand this
for me this is something new

Pulling pieces of me together again
from a dark love poisoned life

slow to catch up hold on
give me a chance

I am the destination that is worth the wait
Forgive me I am weak

recovering from last years heartbreak

Fragile
A chance this is to repair me

Chance (cont'd)

Heart needs to grow
feel again

I need your band-aid of love
It will make me whole again

Take a chance on me
I will try not to crash and burn

So, Flawed

Palm of my hand lay something special
so delicate and fragile, see through
Something started,
brand new
I wanted it
I take it then choke,
all of it goes up in smoke
Not sure what it is that I do
I sabotage it, and make it turn blue
Grab it, and manage it rough
shake it, till it falls into dust
This is what I do,
myself I cannot trust
Something inside will not let me go
A flaw, and I bomb,
why do I do these things,
I keep thinking
But I cannot do any better
A possibility of a treasure,
yet its so light, just like a feather
But its so powerful, it takes prisoner
my mind, the poison,
its undoing
Overthinking every good thing,
so flawed,
mind

House to Build

I need to build a place

Where no one will kick me out

a house made of trust

foundation built, brick by brick with

Joined with concrete love

construction ripping the ceiling out

Of past mistakes

fortify the heart door with passion

Keeps it solid

windows into the soul
looking in

A house, a place to call home

fortified

I run my hands down these memory walls

remember the sunlight pouring in

Warmth brimming in

I woke up in my head

Candle

Like a dimly lit candle in the dark

My ultimate spark

Wax dripping like tears

Building up for years

The wick is getting low

You always are a flicker in my head

Warm glow

Always a light in the darkness

Hot to the touch,

a burning desire

My one truest sense of light to carry me

My Pencil

My Pencil, has　　　much to do
Draft a novel or　　the next poem
This pencil, it will write　a love letter to someone
This pencil, in my hand　let it create a sketch,　a plan
My pencil, is an　　　extension of me
My pencil, knows the secrets　of only I want it to see
when angered I write a heated　note then throw it
away
My pencil, is my　　trusted companion,
here it lays in wait for the next masterpiece
For the　　next mistake
Ready to create with passion in wake
This pencil, is sharper than a dagger,
it can stop fights or light a love
My pencil, attached to my heart
words written in soul blood,
me

Child

Come with me now
Let me show you the way
Walk with me, show you the lessons I learned
Walk with me, let me give you my eyes to see
Walk with me, investigate my past
in hopes you can see clearly
The things that make me, me,
and not fall into the same destiny
Its the mistakes that made this path
It is the lessons that fixed, I grew
but still, I learn, and so will you
Walk the path that suits your future self,
take you by the hand
See now how strong I am from the path's past
My children, please learn from the error of my ways
I will be there to help, but not always
Walk with me, until your confidence is strong,
wisdom in the pathway of your growth
Your choice to decide
Walk with me, or walk alone, my child
I will love you, no matter what you seek
My very breath is a lesson for you to take

Just Be

Sing like no one is watching

Live, like no one cares

Judge only yourself

Live, but be generous and simple

Love others, but be thoughtful

Kindness, it is in fashion

Peace, is the root
Be protective,

sound of mind

Free to dance and smile, like the sun

Happiness is an air that only you create

Kiss deeply but only with,
passion it its wake

Live content

Grateful for every moment

Raise the vibration
Flow

Just be

Lips

So plump,
so beautiful the shape
So perfect, yet rarely singled out
The window of knowledge, or the window of pain
Paint them in whatever colour
Make them stand out
Accent the face, and shine it with gloss
Chapped and ripped, when exposed to wind
Sun beams on them, soon, they fade
That lustrous pink, its so delicate
Yet they sometimes, tremble in fear
Quiver, in anticipation for touch
Thin out with age, they are now wise
In death, they pale and turn blue
Lips, are the entrance to our soul
The ambassador for our face

Care

Care for you innocent and pure
Care for hearts that are small yet so big
Care for tiny hands that grip fingers strong
Care for beautiful eyes that look at you with wonder
Care for the arms that ache to hold you
Care for the tiny tears that fall when you cry
Care for the little minds that grow at a wondrous pace
with awe
I will care for you, my children; I will always love you.

Wolf

He hides his fangs in his smile
His eyes are yellow filled with hate
He talks to you like a sheep in wolves clothing
in secret you give him a bad taste
He bites your mind with doubts, so you cannot see
Fills your heart with distrust
Tries so desperately to weaken you
He is jealous of you 'because you are pure of heart
Everyone likes you, and he hates it
Laying in wait for your weakest point
Disguises his intention and then cuts you with his teeth
Makes you feel small, so he can consume you
Tries to obliterate you
His fur is like a silk you cannot see his ways
so smooth his words that he speaks
He flows to follow you in hopes you let him in
Now you must hunt him
stop him from destroying you
his bite gripping on to you
All the poison running out of him
Exposed of who he is now you must run
get away from the wolf who is a demon

Power

I am power
I am alive
Powers
It is the mind
Unwavering brain never compromised
Powerful eyes can see
all that is good or bad its more of a feeling
A Power it comes from within
The power to win
Power to keep going when everything is defying
Power to step up
Power to keep a focus on
I am a powerful tide
Crashing doubt out in the mind sea
Turning over ships of friends who do not believe in me
Power like thunder on a dark night
Lighting up the beast and banishing uncertainty
Power like the sun
strong bright and free

His Ending

Thought you and I were one
blended intertwined, one of a kind
Heart now broken
 bleeding out
I, lost
I cannot confide in you
his ending is now my scar
Something is missing it has gone already
 even when I think of you
All I have left is the lies you told
Now I need to feel angry
need to feel tall
Spew words out so I will not feel this at all
Loss is what left
From the time spent
your ending is my new beginning
even if I cannot see it yet

Strong Enough

Strong enough to see it through
Strong enough to get over you
Strong enough to want to be happy
Strong enough to make life better
Strong enough to keep on fighting
Strong enough to fight the nightmare that was you
Strong enough to be strong enough for me
I am strong now
Now and forever strong enough for my children too

LOVE

A Love is something to aspire to
Something to hold on to
Love is all we need
Something that can make us sad when it dies
Love is something to keep
Something to want more than anything
Love, it comes and goes
Something to care for but never grip too tightly
Love can slip through our fingers like sand
Something we cherish but, do not really understand
Love, it graces everyone at one time or another
Something to believe in
Love, it has the power to change lives
Something the world needs more of

Canadian Illustrator / Author Lizy J. Campbell is a self-taught artist. She is a mother of two beautiful children and works from home as an illustrator. She has many interests and currently paints pet portraits, real estate homes and more.

"I love to create. There is no limit to what I want to do, so I keep reaching for the sky. I am enthusiastic about making a difference and making people smile, one creation at a time."